PENCIL, PAPER, DRAW!®
FLOWERS

STEVE HARPSTER

STERLING CHILDREN'S BOOKS
New York

This book is dedicated to my wonderful parents, Charlie and Joann,
who always encouraged me to draw . . . just not during algebra class.

STERLING CHILDREN'S BOOKS
New York

An Imprint of Sterling Publishing
387 Park Avenue South
New York, NY 10016

Previously published in a different format by Sterling Publishing Co., Inc. in 2006.

ISBN 978-1-4549-1154-8

Distributed in Canada by Sterling Publishing
C/o Canadian Manda Group, 165 Dufferin Street
Toronto, Ontario, Canada M6K 3H6
Distributed in the United Kingdom by GMC Distribution Services
Castle Place, 166 High Street, Lewes, East Sussex, England BN7 1XU
Distributed in Australia by Capricorn Link (Australia) Pty. Ltd.
P.O. Box 704, Windsor, NSW 2756, Australia

For information about custom editions, special sales, and premium and corporate purchases, please contact
Sterling Special Sales at 800-805-5489 or specialsales@sterlingpublishing.com.

Manufactured in China
Lot #:
2 4 6 8 10 9 7 5 3 1
02/14

www.sterlingpublishing.com/kids

Contents

Introduction . . . . Page 5

How to Use This Book . . . . Page 6

Flower Facts . . . . Page 8

Draw a Bluebell . . . . Page 10

Draw Daisies . . . . Page 12

Draw Chrysanthemums . . . . Page 14

Draw a Black-eyed Susan . . . . Page 16

Draw a Clematis . . . . Page 18

Draw a Portulaca . . . . Page 19

Draw a Geranium . . . . Page 20

Draw a Mum . . . . Page 22

Draw an Apple Tree Blossom . . . . Page 24

Draw a Columbine . . . . Page 26

Draw a Gazania . . . . Page 28

Draw a Crocus . . . . Page 30

Draw a Pear Tree Blossom . . . . Page 32

Draw a Morning Glory. Page 34

Draw a Daffodil. . . . . Page 36

Draw a Sunflower . . . . Page 38

Draw a Lotus Flower . . . . Page 40

Draw a Carnation. Page 42

Draw an Iris. . . . . Page 44

Draw a Magnolia. . . . . Page 46

Draw an Orchid . . . . Page 48

Draw a Peony . . . . Page 50

Draw a Zinnia. . . . . Page 52

Draw a Poppy . . . . Page 54

Draw a Rose. . . . . Page 56

Draw a Dahlia. . . . . Page 58

Draw a Water Lily . . . . Page 60

Draw a Tulip . . . . Page 62

About the Artist . . . . Page 64

Introduction

Drawing is a lot of fun and a great hobby. You can draw alone or with friends. Draw while watching television or quietly in the library at school. Take a pad of paper and some pencils on a long car trip to pass the time. Keep in mind that drawing is just like playing music, sports, or learning state capitals, it takes practice. Don't expect to be great on the first try. You will learn more and more each time you draw. By putting the date on the bottom or back of your drawings, you can keep track of your progress. Hang your drawings up in your room so you can look at them and see what you can improve on. Just have fun drawing and you will see your drawing skills improve each day.

How to Use This Book

You will notice there are different colored lines in each drawing step. Blue lines are the new steps. Black lines are the lines done in a previous step.

new lines

lines in final drawing

When you first start drawing make sure to draw very light. Many of the shapes and lines you start with are guides and will not be needed in the finished drawing.

You don't need to erase the gray lines in each step as you draw. In the final step press harder with your pencil and trace over the lines you want to keep. You can even go over the final step with a black pen.

A trick that most artists use when drawing is a sheet of tracing paper. Sketch your drawing following the steps in the book. When you are finished, lay a sheet of tracing paper over your finished sketch. Now trace over the lines you want to keep in your final drawing.

 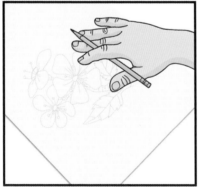  

After following the steps in this book, try drawing something that's not in this book. You should learn to view animals, people, or machines as a group of many shapes and lines. When you begin to see how simple shapes and lines combine to create form, you will be well on your way to drawing anything you want. I hope you have fun learning to draw, and remember, practice makes perfect.

Flower Facts

Parts of a Flower

Humans and animals are made up of many different body parts. Head, torso, legs, and arms are just a few examples of the parts that come together to form a complete body. Flowers are also made up of different parts that create their form. As you draw the flowers in this book, you'll notice how every flower has similar parts, even though they might look different. Some flowers have long stems while others look like they have no stems at all. One flower might have many petals, and another flower will only have four. Understanding the parts of the flower will allow you to draw them correctly.

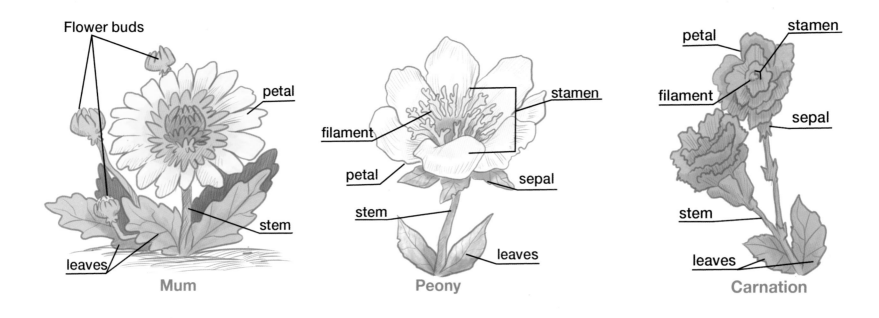

Mum

Peony

Carnation

What flowers don't look like   Geranium

Everyone has drawn a quick picture of a flower. Most people draw flowers like the first two pictures on the top of this page. A perfect circle for the center and some evenly placed petals around the circle. That's fine for a quick drawing of a flower, but it's not really what a flower looks like. Flowers are not perfect shapes, and no two flowers are identical. The petals of a flower each have a different shape. Some of the petals might curl in a different direction, or chunks may be missing from a few bug bites. Not only are the shapes of flower petals different, but the color can vary from petal to petal.

Once you have drawn the individual flowers in this book, try drawing groups of flowers together. You can draw several of the flowers to make an arrangement in a vase or a beautiful flower pot. Go crazy and draw an entire garden with your favorite flowers and color them in any color you want. Just have fun and you can't go wrong.

Draw a Bluebell

1

2

3

4

5

6

7

8

9

10

10

11

12

13

14

15

Draw Daisies

1   2   3   4   5

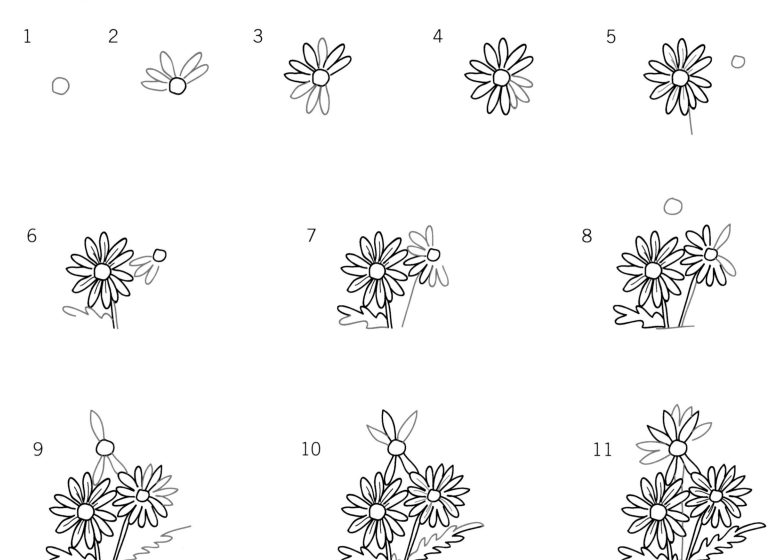

6   7   8

9   10   11

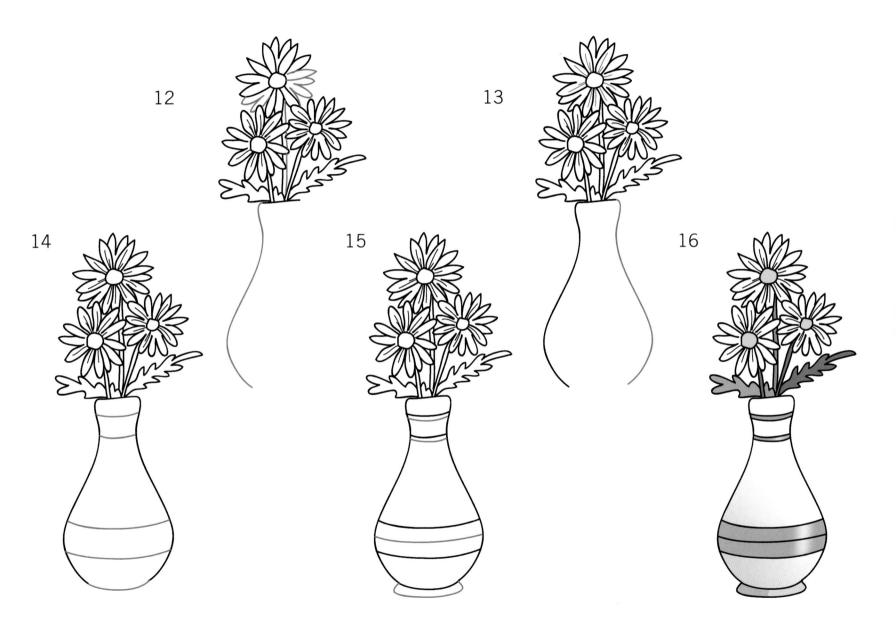

Draw Chrysanthemums

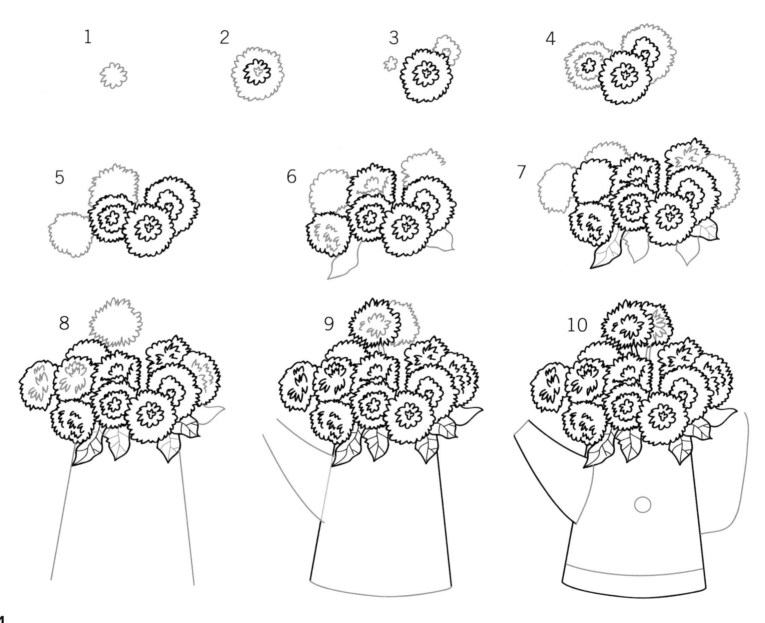

1

2

3

4

5

6

7

8

9

10

11

12

13

14

Draw a Black-eyed Susan

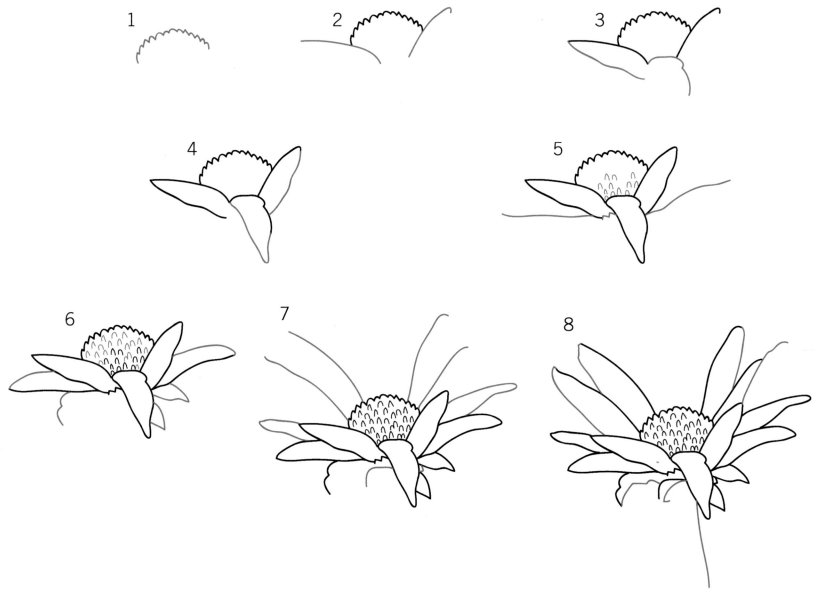

9

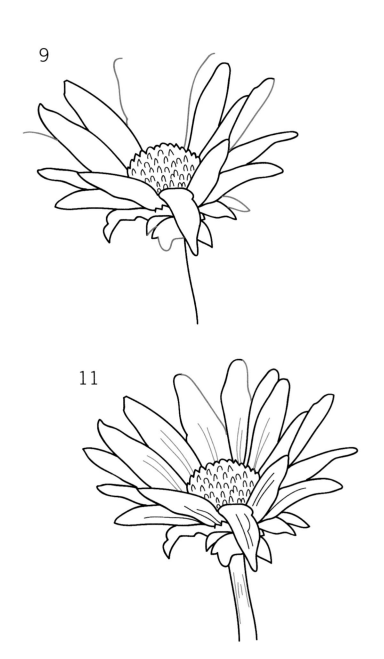

10

11

12

17

Draw a Clematis

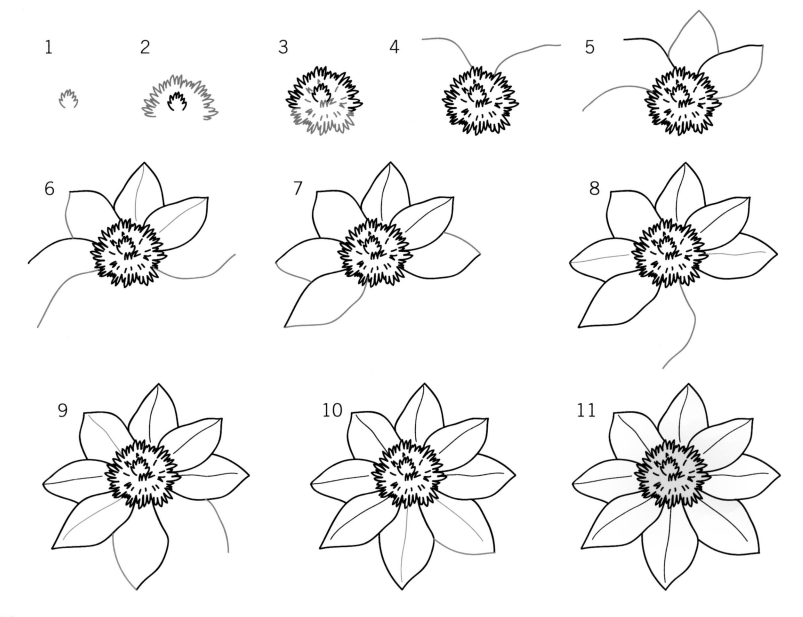

1
2
3
4
5
6
7
8
9
10
11

Draw a Portulaca

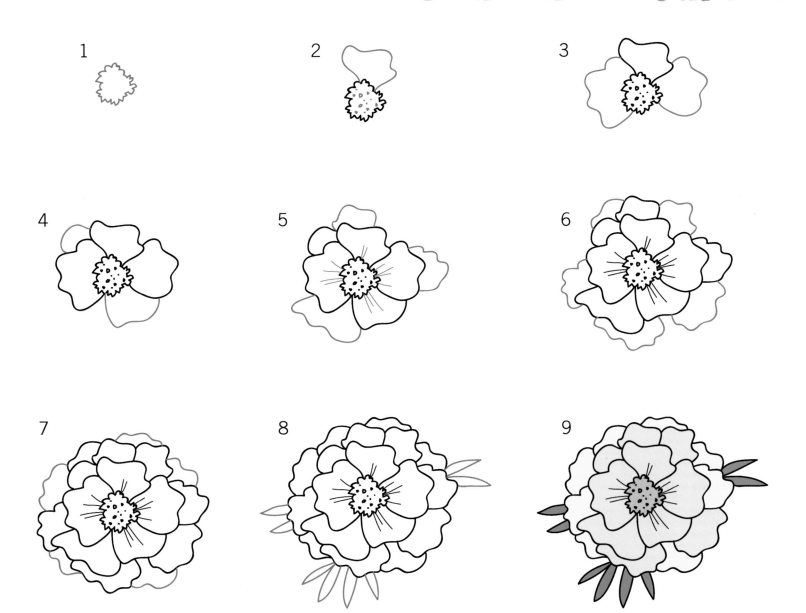

1
2
3
4
5
6
7
8
9

19

Draw a Geranium

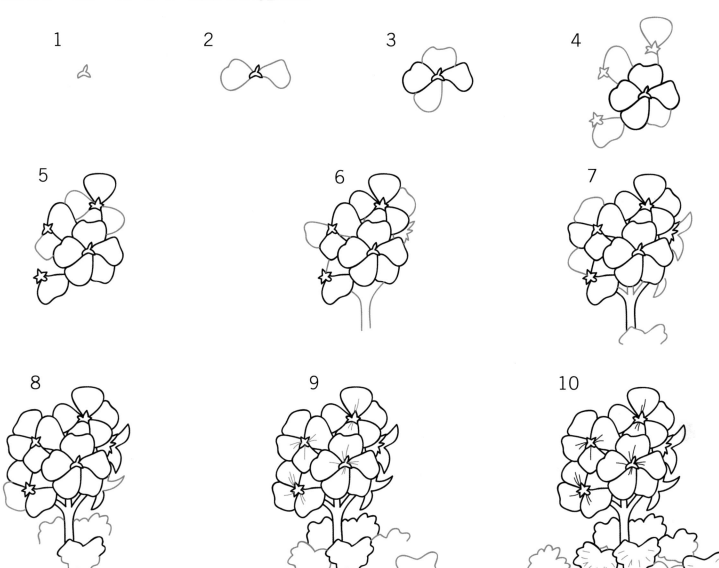

1

2

3

4

5

6

7

8

9

10

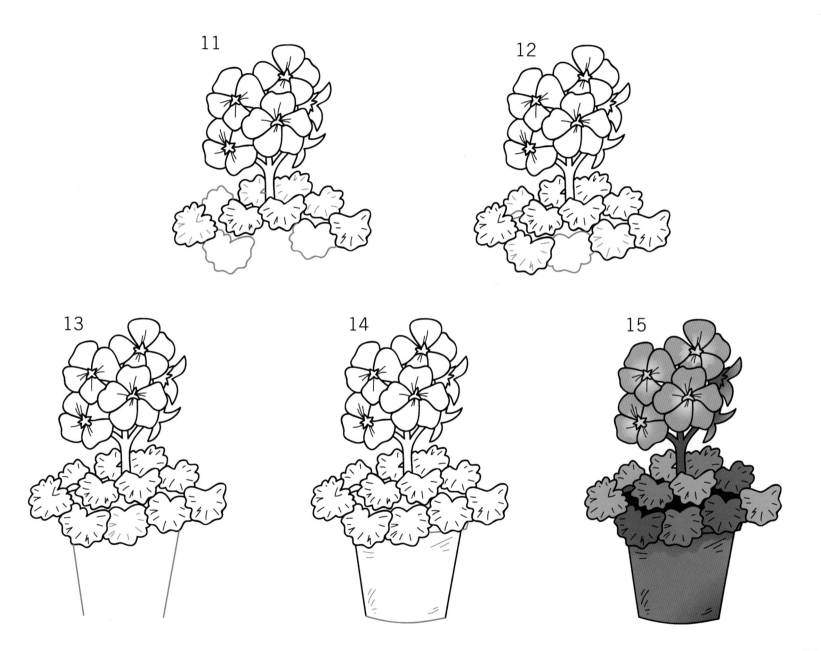

11

12

13

14

15

Draw a Mum

1   2   3   4   5   6
7   8   9
10   11   12

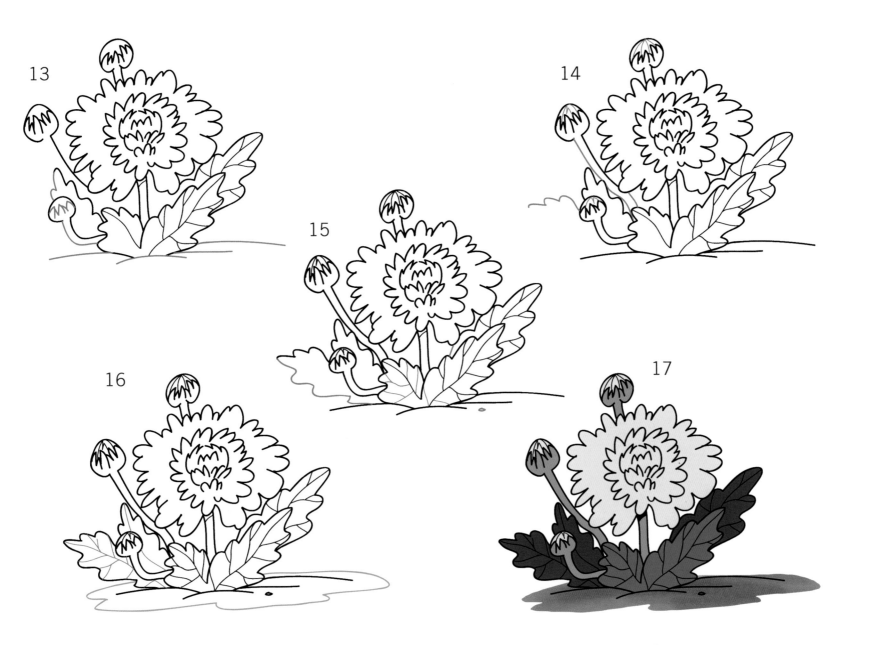

13

14

15

16

17

Draw an Apple Tree Blossom

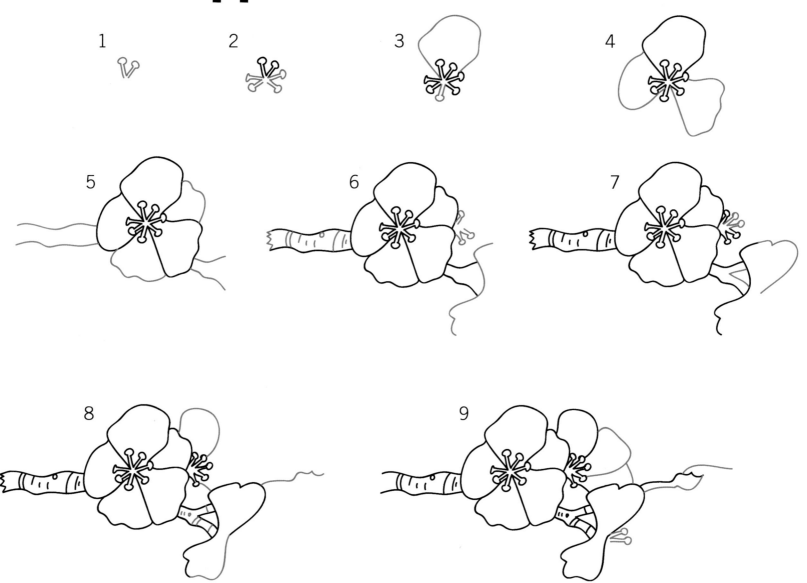

1

2

3

4

5

6

7

8

9

24

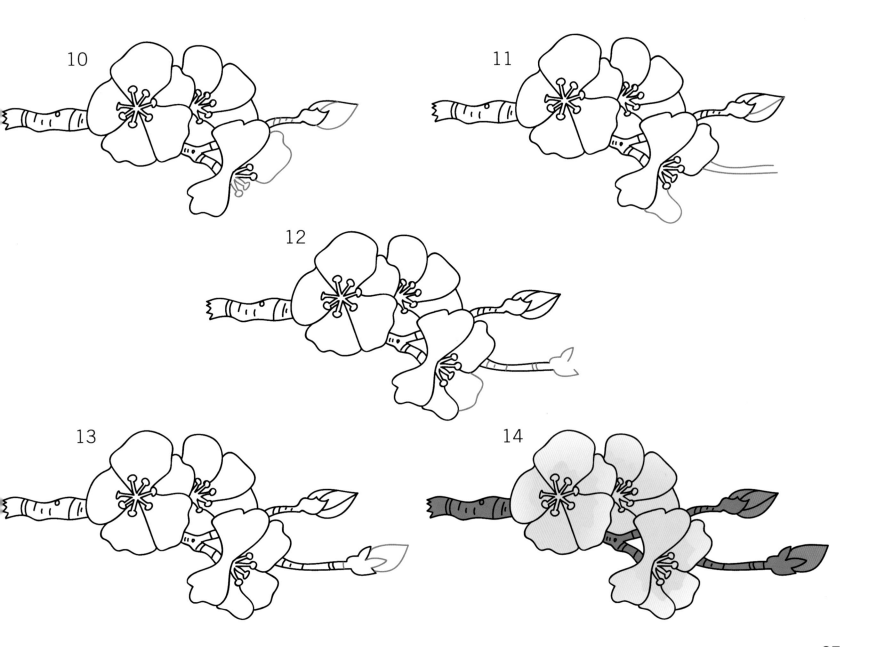

10

11

12

13

14

Draw a Columbine

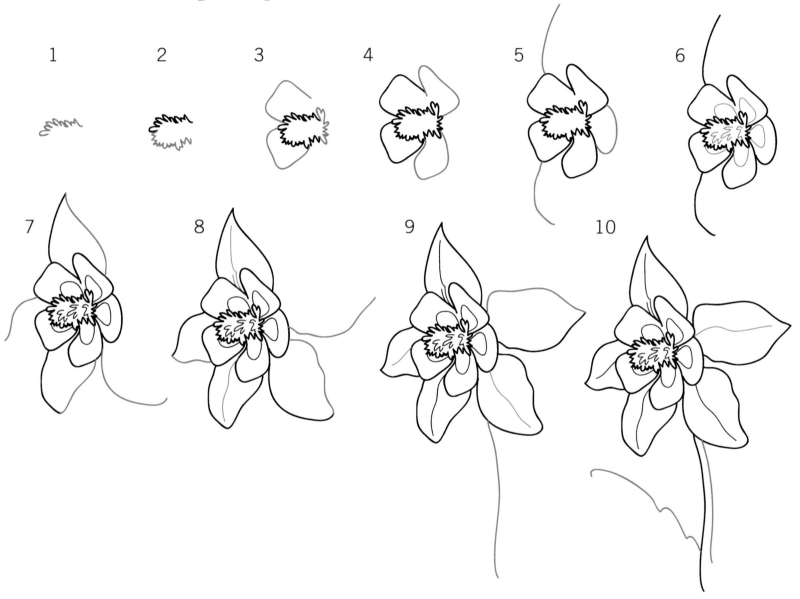

1 2 3 4 5 6

7 8 9 10

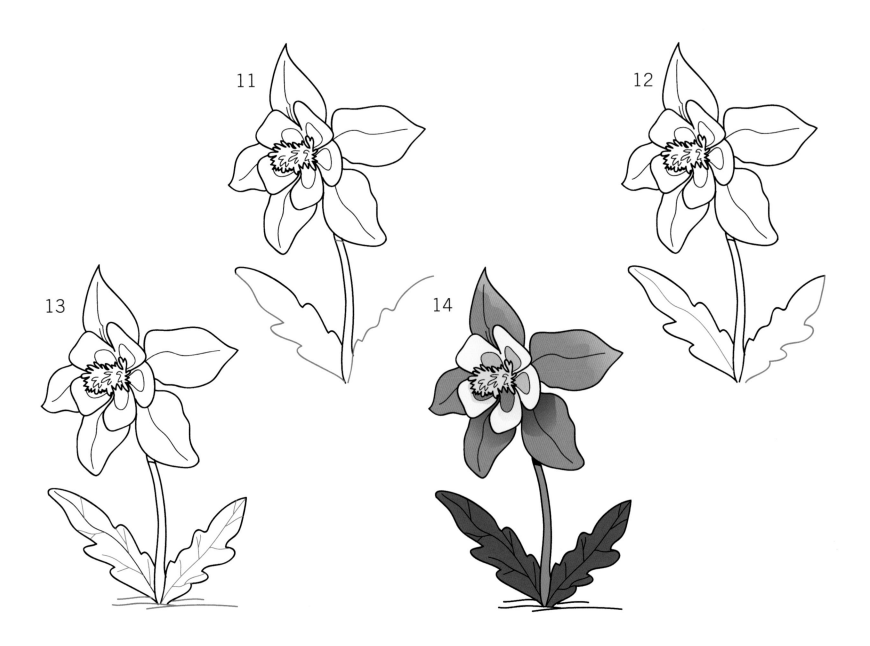

Draw a Gazania

1

2

3

4

5

6

7

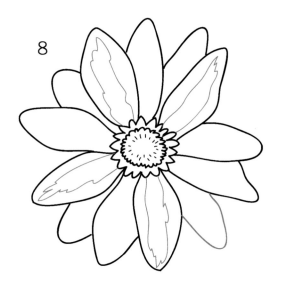

8

9

10

11

Draw a Crocus

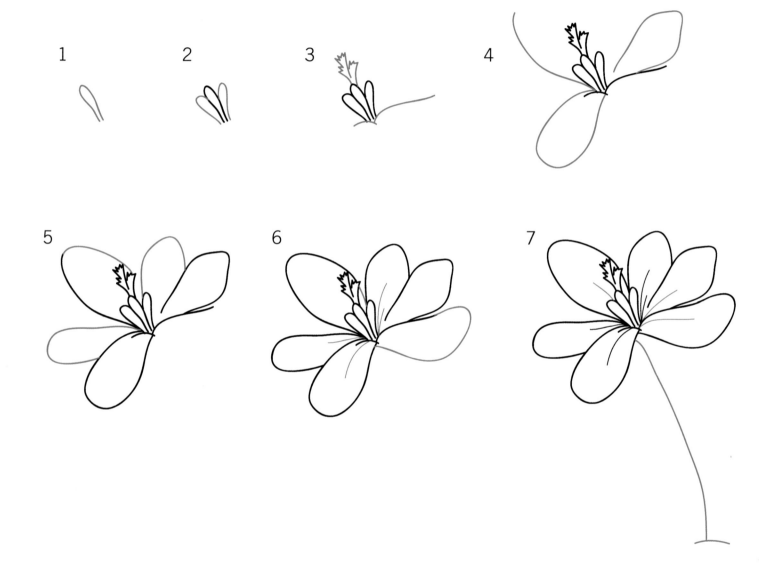

1

2

3

4

5

6

7

30

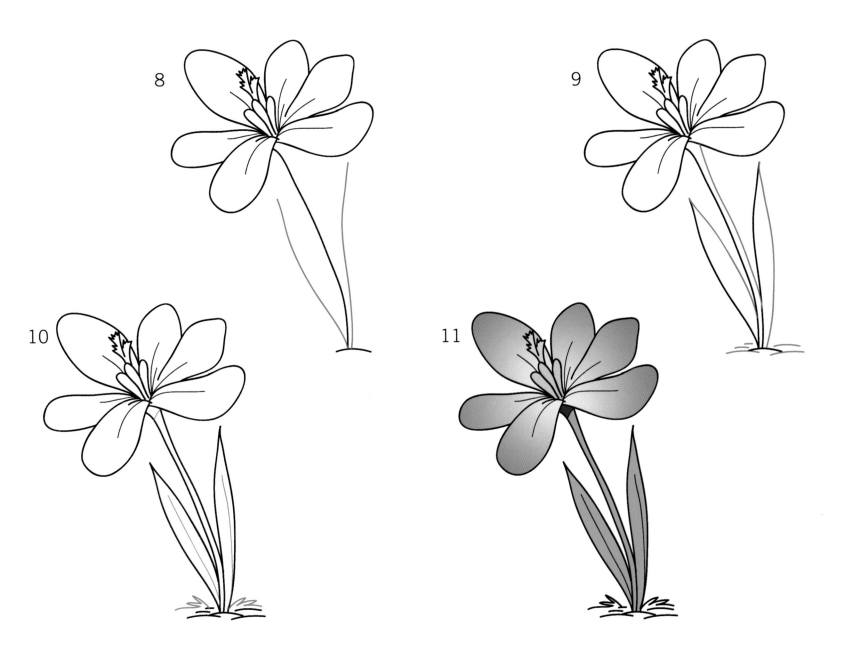

8   9   10   11

Draw a Pear Tree Blossom

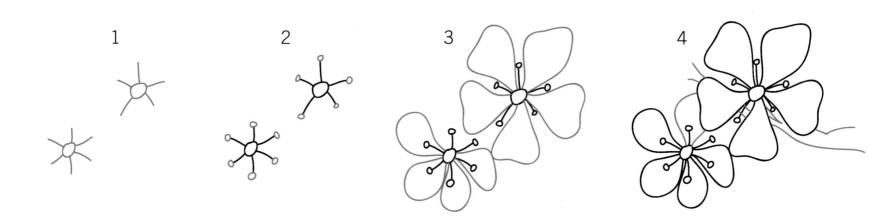

5

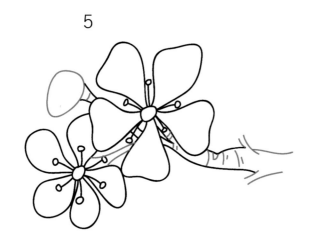

6

7

8

9

10

Draw a Morning Glory

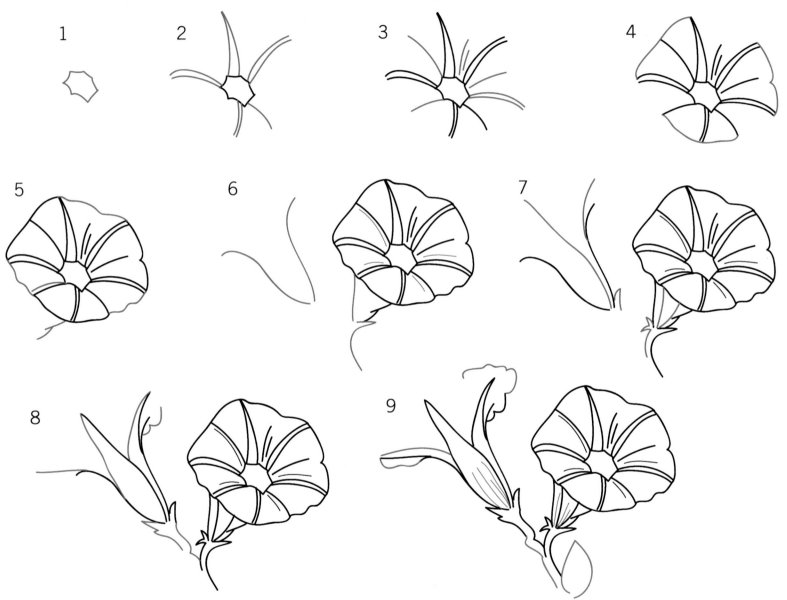

1

2

3

4

5

6

7

8

9

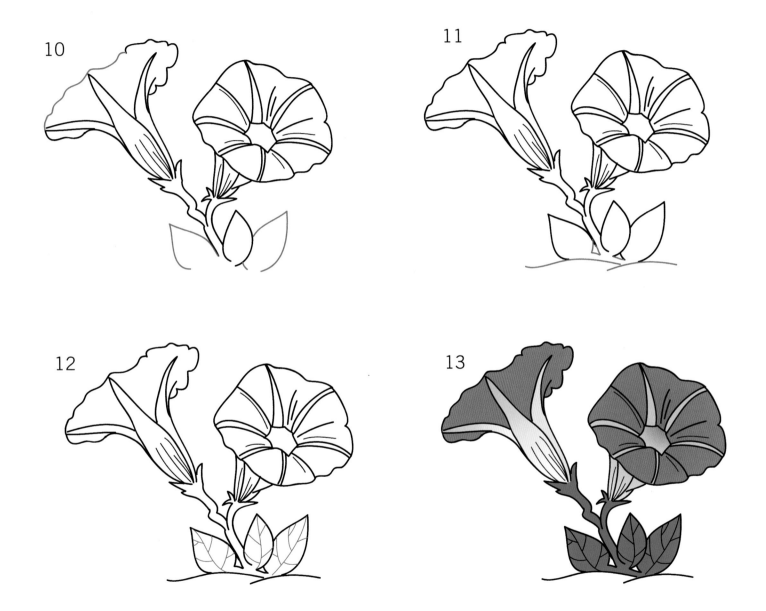

Draw a Daffodil

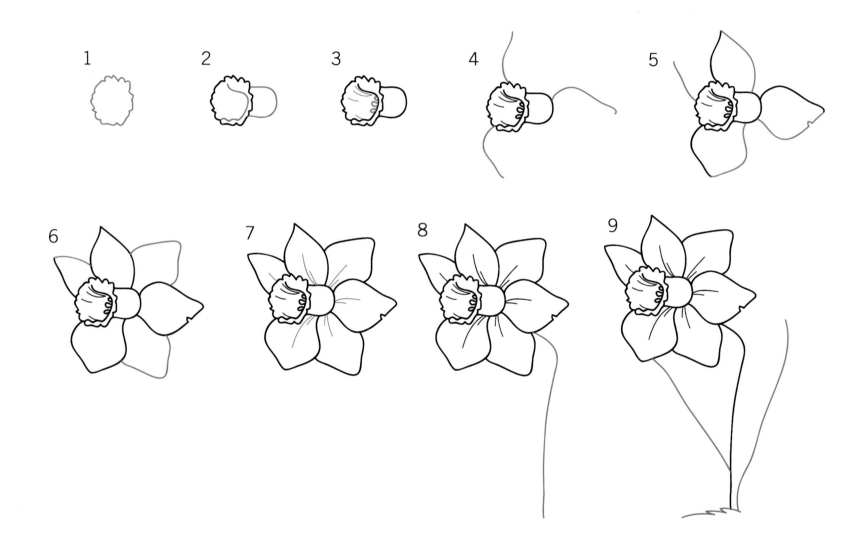

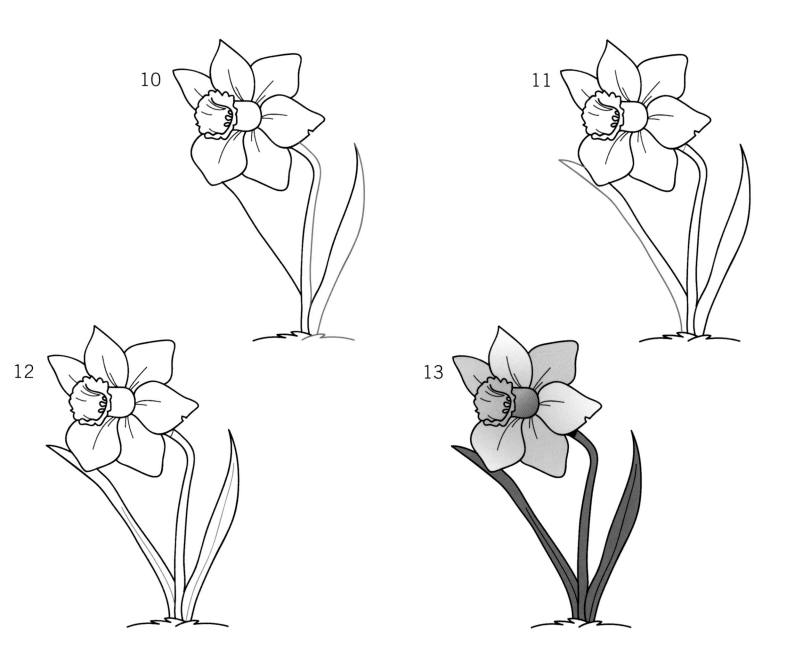

10

11

12

13

Draw a Sunflower

1   2   3   4   5

6   7   8

Draw a Lotus Flower

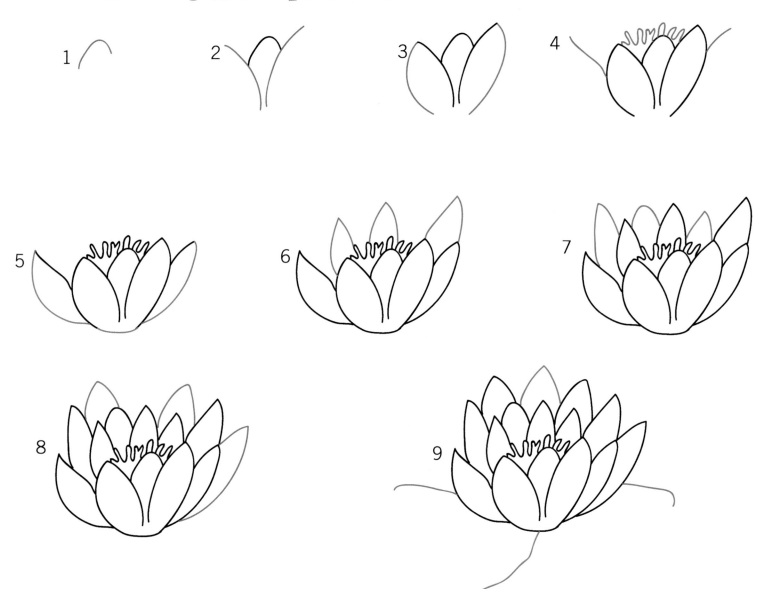

1

2

3

4

5

6

7

8

9

Draw a Carnation

1

2

3

4

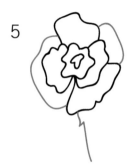

5

6

7

8

9

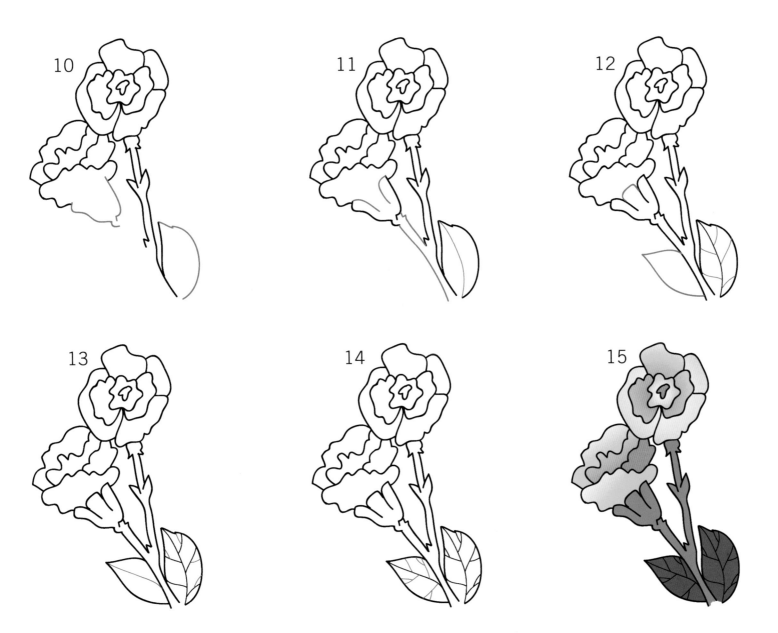

Draw an Iris

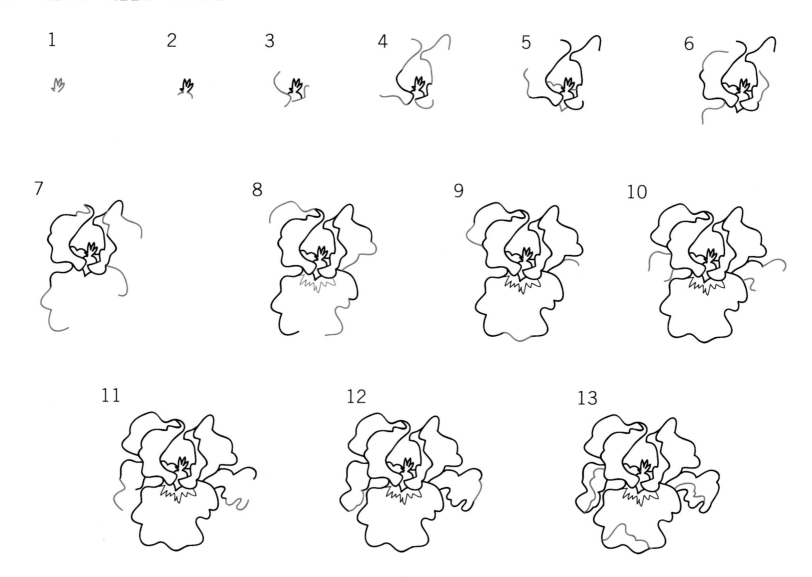

14

15

16

17

18

19

Draw a Magnolia

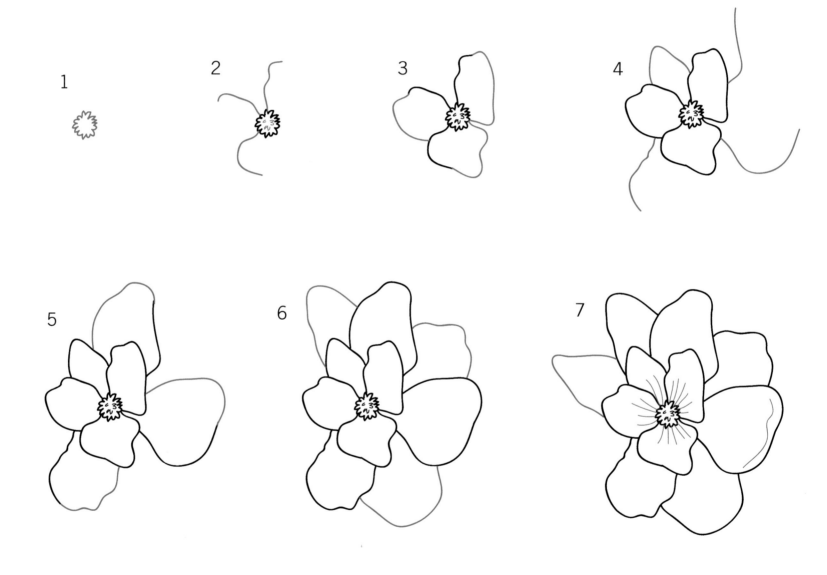

1

2

3

4

5

6

7

8

9

10

11

Draw an Orchid

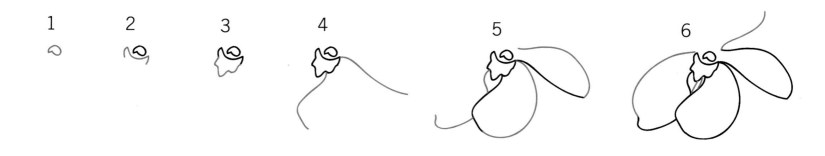

1 2 3 4 5 6

7

8

9

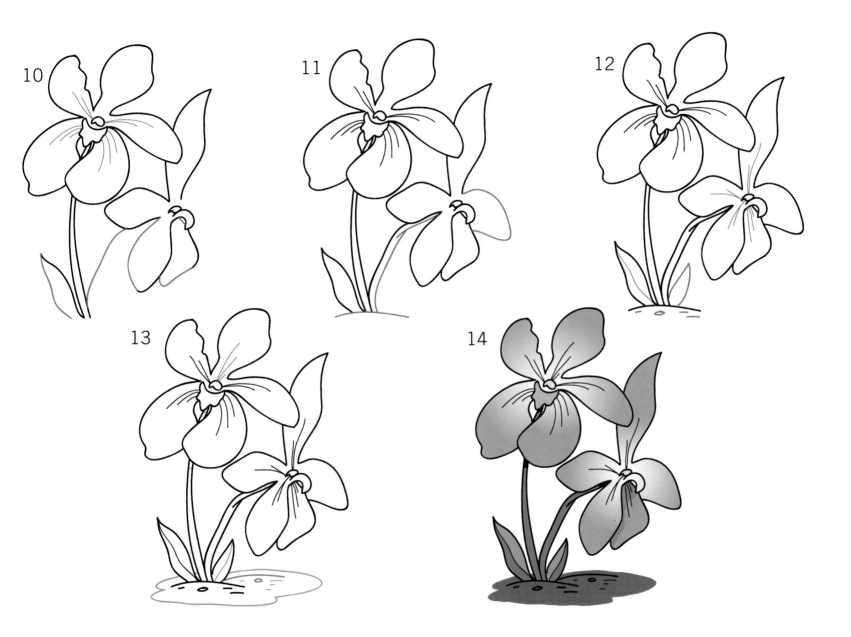

Draw a Peony

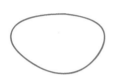

1

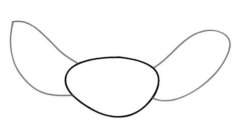

2

3

4

5

6

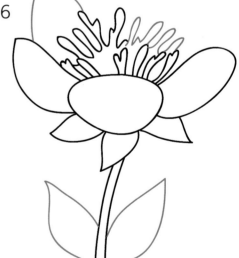

7

8

9

10

51

Draw a Zinnia

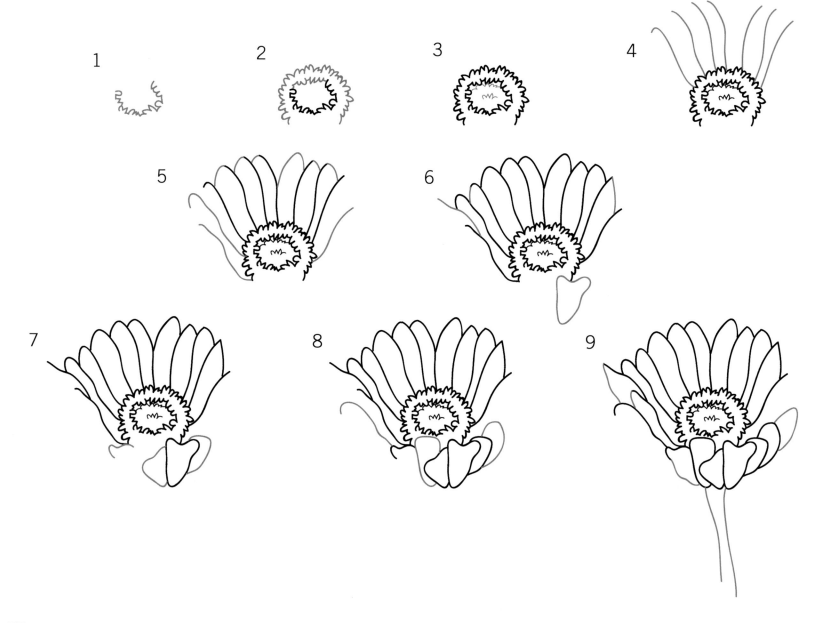

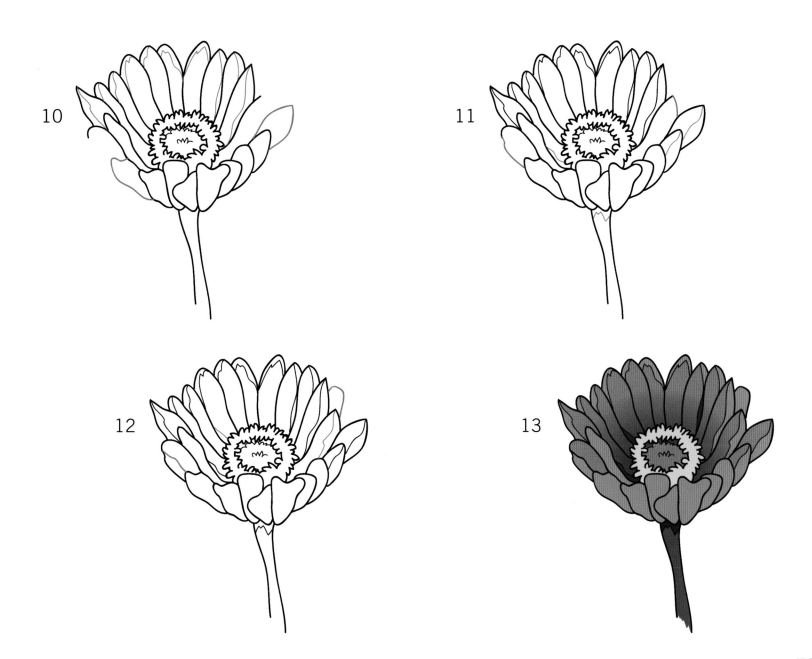

Draw a Poppy

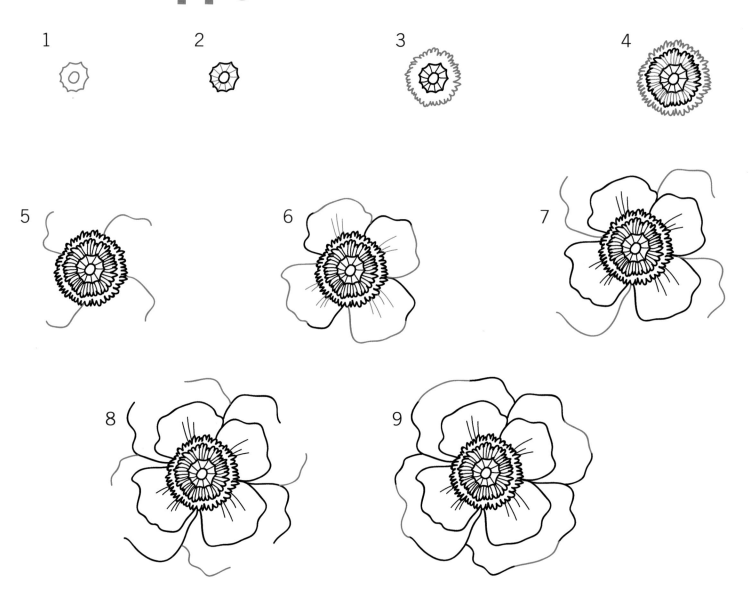

1

2

3

4

5

6

7

8

9

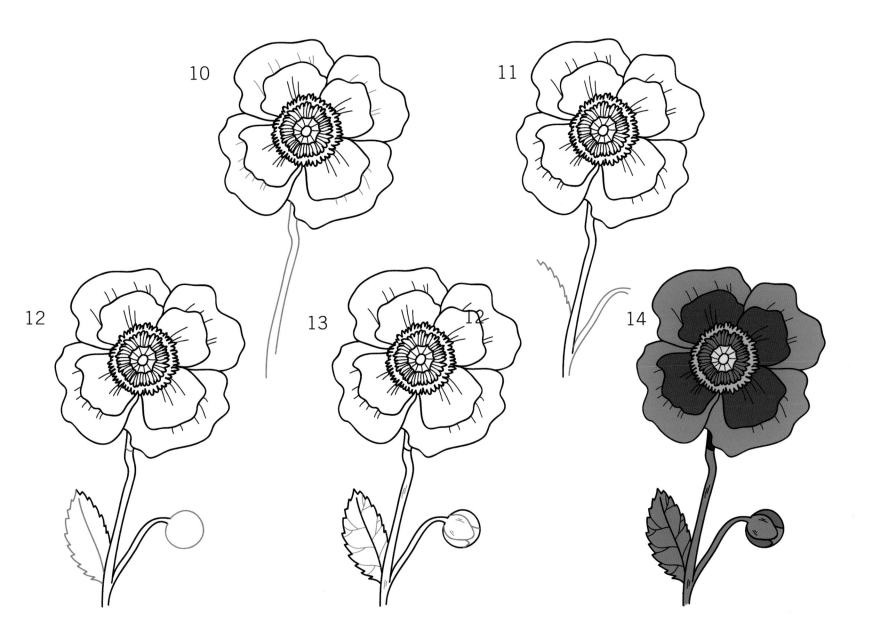

10

11

12

13

12

14

Draw a Rose

1

2

3

4

5

6

7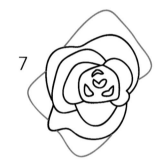

8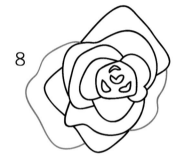

9

10

11

12

13

14

15

Draw a Dahlia

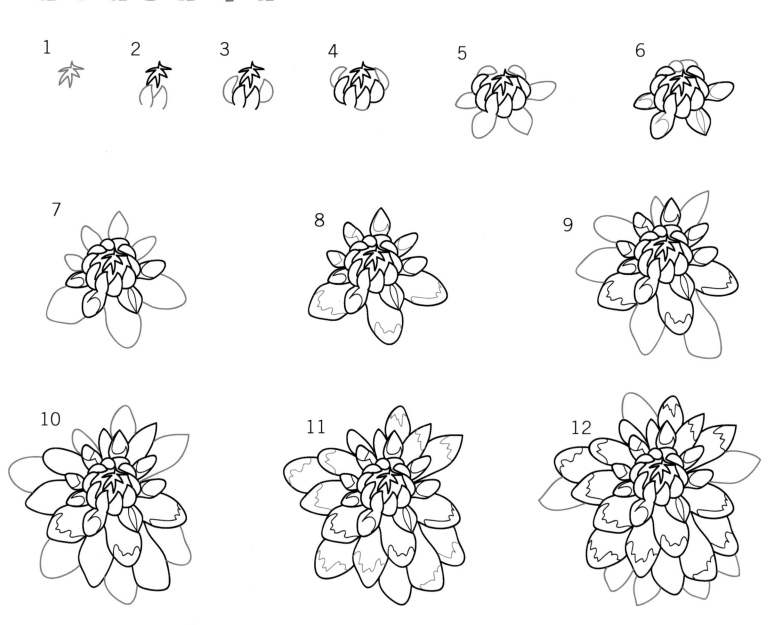

1
2
3
4
5
6
7
8
9
10
11
12

13

14

15

16

17

Draw a Water Lily

1

2

3

4

5

6

7

8

9

10

11

12

Draw a Tulip

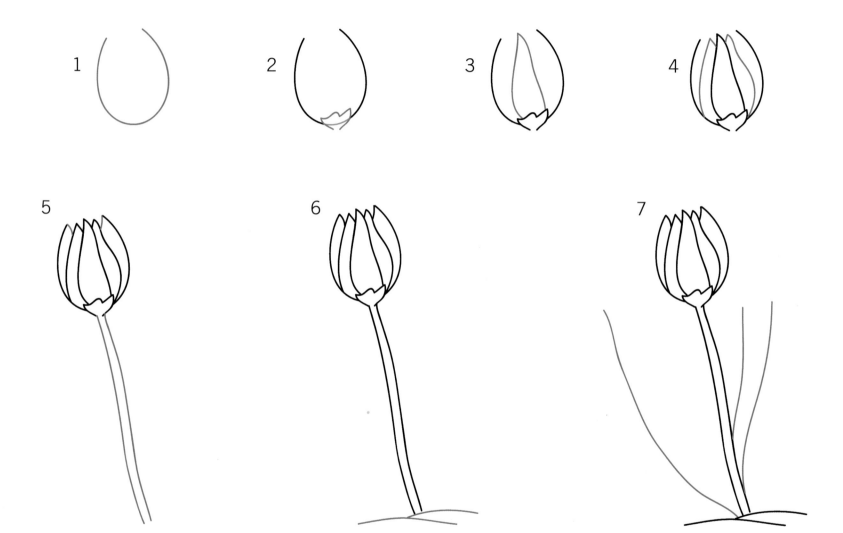

8

9

10

About the Artist

Steve's interest in drawing was sparked in first grade and continued all through his school years. After graduating from Capital University with a Bachelor of Fine Arts degree, Steve worked for various companies as an artist before finally deciding to head off on his own and work as a freelance illustrator. Steve has been working as a freelance illustrator for over ten years now and has over 50 children's books to his credit. He currently lives with his lovely wife, Karen, and his sheepdog, Doodle, in Columbus, Ohio.

Other Pencil, Paper, Draw!® **books to look for:**

. . . .

Pencil, Paper, Draw!® **ANIMALS**
Pencil, Paper, Draw!® **BABY ANIMALS**
Pencil, Paper, Draw!® **CARS & TRUCKS**
Pencil, Paper, Draw!® **DINOSAURS**
Pencil, Paper, Draw!® **DOGS**
Pencil, Paper, Draw!® **FANTASY CREATURES**
Pencil, Paper, Draw!® **HORSES**
Pencil, Paper, Draw!® **PIRATES**
Pencil, Paper, Draw!® **SHARKS**

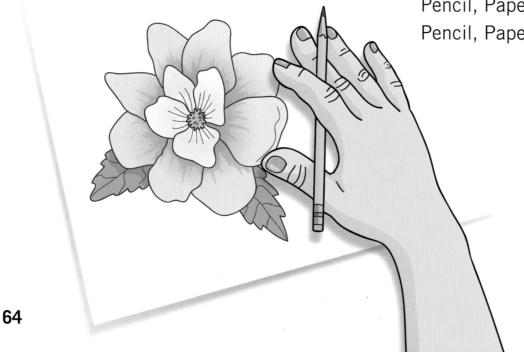